SHARKS

Sarah Creese

make
believe
ideas

Sleek sharks are short and long,
large and fast and fierce and strong.
Beware the pointed, big shark fin,
a powerful tail and a toothy grin!

SHARKS

Reading together

This book is an ideal first reader for your child, combining simple words and sentences with stunning colour photography of real-life sharks. Here are some of the many ways you can help your child take those first steps in reading. Encourage your child to:

- Look at and explore the detail in the pictures.
- Sound out the letters in each word.
- Read and repeat each short sentence.

Look at the pictures

Make the most of each page by talking about the pictures and spotting key words. Here are some questions you can use to discuss each page as you go along:

- Why do you like this shark?
- What is special about it?
- Where does it live?
- What does it eat?

Look at rhymes

Some of the sentences in this book are simple rhymes. Encourage your child to recognise rhyming words. Try asking the following questions:

- What does this word say?
- Can you find a word that rhymes with it?

- Look at the ending of two words that rhyme. Are they spelled the same? For example, "meal" and "seal", and "teeth" and "reef".

Test understanding

It is one thing to understand the meaning of individual words, but you need to check that your child understands the facts in the text.

- Play "spot the obvious mistake". Read the text as your child looks at the words with you, but make an obvious mistake to see if he or she catches it. Ask your child to correct you and provide the right word.

- After reading the facts, shut the book and make up questions to ask your child.

- Make statements about the sharks and ask your child whether the statements are true or false.

- Provide your child with three answers to a question and ask him or her to pick the correct one.

Quiz pages

At the end of the book there is a simple quiz. Ask the questions and see if your child can remember the right answers from the text. If not, encourage him or her to look up the answers.

Sharks

Amazing sharks live in oceans around the world.

With a mouth full of sharp
teeth, sharks are deadly
hunters of the sea.

I'm a great white shark.
I'm white and grey.
A strong sense of smell,
helps me hunt my prey.

Splash!

With sharp, pointed teeth,
I catch a meal –
some fish, a sea lion,
whale or seal!

Did you know?

Sharks have many rows of teeth
in their mouth. When a tooth gets
damaged, another tooth is
ready to replace it.

Did you know?

Tiger sharks take their name from the tiger-like patterns they have when they are young.

I'm a tiger shark,
I like to hunt alone.
My tiger stripes will fade,
when I'm fully grown.

I'm a shark
with a rectangular head.
I attack stingrays
on the seabed!

Did you know?

Hammerheads' eyes are wide apart. This helps them to see more than other sharks.

I'm the world's largest fish,
but I'm as harmless as can be.
I'm a massive whale shark.
There's none bigger than me.

17

I rest in the day
with other nurse sharks.
When night-time comes,
I hunt in the dark!

Did you know?

Nurse sharks live in warm,
shallow water. They swim slowly
at the bottom of the sea.

With long, thin teeth,
I eat my favourite dish,
a tasty meal of
wriggly reef fish.

Did you know?

Divers, snorkellers and swimmers often see the blacktip reef shark.

I swim smoothly
around the coral reef.
Look out for my black fins
and super, sharp teeth.

You might find me swimming
in a muddy or sandy bay.
My body is covered with
dots of brown and grey.

Did you know?

Zebra sharks only have spots when they are older. When they are young, they are covered in stripes instead!

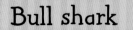

I'm a powerful bull shark.
My snout is short and blunt.
Shallow water and rivers
are where I like to hunt!

Did you know?

The bull shark has been known
to bump other sharks and divers
if it thinks they are both trying
to catch the same prey!

What do you know?

1. Which shark is the largest fish in the world?

2. Which shark's snout is short and blunt?

3. When does a nurse shark hunt?

4. What pattern does a young zebra shark have on its body?

5. What shape is a hammerhead shark's head?

6. In what type of water does a nurse shark live?

7. What colour is a great white shark?

8. Which shark can hunt in rivers?

9. What pattern does an adult zebra shark have on its body?

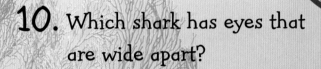

10. Which shark has eyes that are wide apart?

11. What do great white sharks like to eat?

12. Which shark likes to swim around the coral reef?

Answers

1. The whale shark. 2. The bull shark. 3. Nurse sharks hunt at night.
4. It is covered in stripes. 5. It is rectangular. 6. Nurse sharks live in warm, shallow water. 7. Grey and white. 8. The bull shark.
9. It is covered in grey and brown dots. 10. The hammerhead shark.
11. Fish, sea lions, whales or seals. 12. The blacktip reef shark.

Dictionary

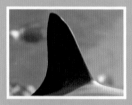

fin
Fish have fins to help them swim, steer and balance.

stingray
A stingray is a flat fish with a long tail. It can be found at the bottom of the seabed.

hunt
To hunt another animal is to chase and eat it.

pointed
Things that are pointed get thinner towards their tip. They can also be sharp.

blunt
If something is blunt it does not have a sharp point.

Key words

Here are some key words used in context.
Make simple sentences for the other
words in the border.

I **like** to eat stingrays.

I swim smoothly.

My teeth are sharp.

I **have** a stripy body.

I am **the** largest fish.

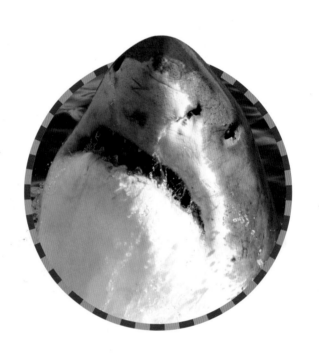